Even More Little Stories for Little Children

Even More Little Stories for Little Children

A Worship Resource

Donna McKee Rhodes

Herald
Press

Scottdale, Pennsylvania
Waterloo, Ontario

Library of Congress Cataloging-in-Publication Data
Rhodes, Donna McKee, 1962-
    Even more little stories for little children : a worship resource/
Donna McKee Rhodes.
        p. cm.
    ISBN 0-8361-9129-3
        1. Children's sermons. 2. Storytelling in Christian
education. I. Title.

BV4315.R45 2000
252'.53—dc21   00-022503

All Bible quotations are used by permission, all rights reserved
and are from the *New Revised Standard Version of the Bible,* copy-
right 1989, by the Division of Christian Education of the
National Council of the Churches of Christ in the USA.

To Loren—

Dedicated church worker;
inspirational teacher;
thoughtful dad;
my partner on life's journey.

Contents

Preface and Acknowledgments

*T*HIS COLLECTION OF STORIES is offered to you in the manner of its predecessors. Use the stories as they are or as starting points for your own inspirations. I hope you will find these offerings meaningful as you minister to children in various settings, whether at home, a worship service, church school class, camp, Christian school, or some other situation.

This collection results from my continued service as Pastor of Nurture at Stone Church of the Brethren. Each message is designed to be in coordination with a Scripture and worship theme.

I am grateful to the people of Stone Church of the Brethren. In my ten years there, beginning as a lay person who coordinated Christian education and continuing with a call to set-apart ministry, my love and care for my church family has grown. Their ongoing encouragement for my ministry and writing projects has been inspirational. Robert W. Neff, in particular, has been a great support through his Scripture consultation. And the congregation's children inspire as they eagerly gather for their special worship time.

Certainly my books would not be realities without the help of special people. Loren, my husband, provides encouragement, a listening ear, and invaluable computer advice. Our children Erica, Aaron, and Joel are patient when I need solitary writing time; and they provide ideas when my creativity feels low.

Herald Press is a fine organization. I am thankful to S. David Garber for his encouragement and support. I am grateful also for the fine marketing process at Herald Press. Without that, these collections would not be reaching across the world. And I am grateful to have had opportunity to work one more time with Michael A. King, who through Pandora Press U.S. is producing this book for Herald Press. Michael is a dedicated and thoughtful editor who helps to shepherd both the book and the author through the publishing process.

Thank you to the thousands of readers who made the earlier collections successful and who asked for more. Blessings to all of you as you minister to children.

—*Donna McKee Rhodes*
Huntingdon, Pennsylvania

*I*ntroduction

I CONSIDER IT AN HONOR TO SIT on the steps in the sanctuary of Stone Church of the Brethren as the children gather for their special time. As is true in many churches, they come with enthusiasm and a spark that inspires the entire congregation.

A special time for children, whether during a worship service, a church school hour, a camp setting, or devotions in a family home, is a fine way to help children develop a picture of God and to deepen their relationship with God. And it is God who has given us, as pastors, educators, and parents, the incredible responsibility of ministering to the children in our midst.

My hope is that this collection of messages will provide you with ideas and inspiration as you minister to children near you. As I gave careful thought to the themes in each story, I tried to imagine how children would view or relate to the theme. What object or picture would help to make the idea clearer? This tangible object would then move the children from the known (the object) to the unknown (the Scripture idea).

As I developed my own style of "Time with the Children," I discovered that I value the following ideas:

> • I believe it is an honor and a privilege to sit with children during worship and share the Good

News. This is a time for children and the congregation to remember that God's love is for all people no matter what their age, skills, or lifestyle.

- I believe a story time is a wonderful occasion for children to experience love and acceptance. People say children are the church of the future. I agree, but I would also say that children are the church of today. Children minister to us as much as we minister to them. We give them the words, the head knowledge of what being a Christian means. They give us the actions, the heart knowledge of what being a Christian is—the hugs, smiles, joy, the quick compassion.

- I believe that children's time is an opportunity to learn about being a servant. I frequently give the children an item to be shared with someone else.

- I believe children's time should be concise, easy to follow, and contain only one main point.

- I believe the storyteller should nurture self- esteem. Sometimes what the children say is funny and causes the congregation to laugh. While the child's statement might have been funny to adults, it was probably a very serious statement on the part of the child. The storyteller can affirm the child by taking the statement seriously and by giving the child a positive response.

- I believe that each time with the children should close with a simple sentence prayer because this helps children realize that relating to God through prayer is important.

An added feature of this collection is a comprehensive index of Scripture references used in all three collections.

God has given us a wonderful gift in the children of the world. Enjoy the responsibility of mentoring these children. May you be enriched and enlivened as you care for God's children near and far.

1
God's Signature

Theme God gives his signature in a variety of ways
Scripture Genesis 1:26-27
Object Signatures from an adult Sunday school class

DO YOU KNOW WHAT A SIGNATURE IS? It is the signing of your name. Some of you print your name. Some of you write it in cursive. Those of you who are in school know that you need to put your signature on all your schoolwork, so the teacher knows which paper belongs to what student. Our signatures tell other people who we are.

All of the students in my Sunday school class put their signature on this paper today. Do you see how they are all different? Signatures reveal a little bit about us. Some people have messy signatures. Maybe that says they are in a hurry. Some people have very small signatures. Maybe that says they like things neat and orderly. Other people sign their names with fancy writing. They use their pen or pencil to make curls or long lines. Maybe that says they are dreamers or like detailed designs.

Did you know that God has a signature? In fact, God has lots of signatures. We don't see the writing of his signature in letters—G-o-d—but we see God's signatures all around us. God reveals his goodness in the beauty of nature: snow, trees, flowers, and many other things. All of the signs of nature are God's signatures. We see God's signature in people who need our help and concern. We see God's signature in the people around us that care for us and help us. We see God's signature in the good feelings we get as we worship.

There are many places to see God's signature. Open your eyes and ears. Look at and listen to our beautiful world. Look at your family and friends. Think about God, and the blessings God has given us in many signatures!

Let's pray—

Dear God, your beautiful signatures are all around us. Thank you for your blessings, and remind us to look for your signature. Amen.

2

*D*ays of Adventure

New calendar year or new school year
Theme Each day is an adventure with God
Scripture Genesis 24: 50-61
Object Pencil for each child

This story took place the Sunday after school began in the fall. However, it could easily be adapted for the first Sunday in January. Adjust the story for your day. Try to find pencils that have a Bible verse printed on them.

*T*HIS PAST WEEK WAS A TIME of new experiences for many of you. What big event happened? School started! How many of you went to school this week?

We have children of many different ages here this morning. Some of you have been to school before and others of you went for the first time. Some of you go to school at home. Some of you ride a bus. Some of you are in preschool. Some of you can look forward to going to school when you are a little older.

Each day is a piece in God's plan for you. Whether you are at school, at home, or playing with friends; each day is a special day from God. There may be exciting times, scary times, or sad times in your days. But God is with you always.

God is walking with you at home, at school, or when you are playing. You can talk to God whenever you want to, and God will always listen.

Each day is a new beginning. We don't know what will happen, but we do know that God is with us on both the good days and the difficult days. We can look at each day as an adventure with God.

I have a new pencil for each of you. You may use it at school or at home. As you use this pencil, remember that God loves you and God will be with you. May each of your days be an adventure.

Let's pray—

Dear God, thank you for each day. Thank you for your plan for us. Help us to remember that you are with us always. Amen.

3

*M*aking *Choices*

Theme Choices are a part of life
Scripture Joshua 24:14-25
Object Various pairs of unlike objects

*L*ET'S PLAY A GAME THIS morning. In my bag, I have pairs of things. These are things from our everyday life. These pairs show choices you need to make everyday. I am going to show you these pairs of things. Tell me which you would choose. Remember, there is no wrong answer.

First pair: I have an apple and a banana. Who would choose an apple? Who would choose a banana?

Second pair: I have blue shorts and red shorts. Who would choose blue shorts? Who would choose red shorts?

Third pair: I have a ball and a bottle of bubbles. Who would choose to play ball? Who would choose to blow bubbles?

These were choices that weren't too difficult. There are other choices in your life that will be harder. Maybe someday a person will offer you something that is not healthy for your body. Or you will be asked to do something that is wrong. You will need to choose whether to say yes or no.

When you're faced with a difficult choice, stop and think, "What would Jesus want me to do?" Not only can you think about what Jesus would do, you can also pray and ask Jesus to help you be strong and make the right decision.

Let's pray—
Dear God, help us to make the right choices. Guide us, make us strong, and thank you for loving us. Amen.

4
*L*ook to God

Theme Keep your eyes on God
Scripture Deuteronomy 6:4-9
Object Actual sunflowers or pictures of sunflowers

*G*OOD MORNING! I'M GLAD all of you are here this morning. I would like you to see a flower I brought with me. Who knows what the name of this flower is? Yes, sunflower is right. Do you have any idea why it's called a sunflower?

Sunflowers are very popular flowers. They are so pretty, and the seeds are good for people and animals to eat. Sunflowers love the sun! The sunflower looks to the sun all day long.

When the sun rises, the sunflower looks toward it. As the sun travels across the sky, the sunflower tilts to keep looking at the sun. Finally as the sun sets in the west, the sunflower turns so it still faces the sun. The sunflower looks toward the sun at all times.

Like the sunflower that turns and tilts to follow the sun, we should look to God at all times. The love we have for God will make us want to put God first in our hearts. We should think of God as soon as we wake up in the morning. We should remember God all day long. Before we go to bed at night, we should say thank you to God for guidance through the day. When we love and follow God, we are able to share God's love with other people.

Each day we are faced with many decisions. If we remember to look to God and pray for guidance, we can be helpful to others. We can pray to God to help us serve him.

It is important for us to love God with our heart, mind, and soul. We should always look to God, just like the sunflower looks to the sun.

Let's pray—

Dear God, thank you for sunflowers that help to make our world beautiful. Thank you for your love. May we always look to you. Amen.

5
Look for the Little

Theme Little things in our lives are important
Scripture 1 Kings 19:9-14
Object A small creation from an erector set

If you don't have access to an erector set, substitute some-thing that gives the effect of being small.

HOW MANY OF YOU LIKE to build things? We can build with so many things, like blocks, Legos, K'nex, or Tinkertoys. We can build with wood, hammers, and nails.

This morning I would like to show you a little creation that Aaron made just for our time together. These pieces from an erector set are held together with tiny screws. What would happen if I took a screw out of its place? Yes, the pieces would come apart. Let's look at how little this screw is. Wow! It is so tiny!

But this tiny screw is so important! It holds together the pieces. This tiny, but important, screw is a needed part of the creation.

In our lives, sometimes we only think about the biggest and the best things. For example, we think about the big game, the best art project, who will win, or how great something is.

The biggest isn't always the best. We need to keep our eyes open to see little things that are important: a smile, a hug, a friend, a flower, or sunshine. Can you think of any other little things that are important? *(Encourage and welcome the children's responses.)*

God gives us gifts in many ways. Keep your eyes open for those gifts. And remember, you can share little things with other people. When you share a smile or a hug, you are sharing a gift from God.

Let's pray—

Dear God, remind us that the biggest isn't always the best. Little things are important, too. Help us to share important things, both large and small, with other people. Amen.

6
Strong as a Tree

Theme Growing strong through a relationship with God
Scripture Psalm 1
Object Picture of a tree

*H*ELLO! I'M GLAD TO SEE each of you. How many of you have a tree near your house? Trees are special gifts from God. Trees give us oxygen and shade. They give us paper and wood. Depending on the kind of tree, we may get fruit from it.

We can also have fun with trees. We can climb trees, build tree houses, or swing in trees. In the autumn, we can rake the leaves into piles and jump up and down in the leaves.

A tree needs certain things to grow. A tree needs water, sun, and nutrients—food—from the soil. The tree puts its roots down deep into the soil. When windstorms and rainstorms come, the tree can be safe because it has grown strong.

Did you know we are like trees? We need things to grow. We need food for our bodies. We learn and study to be strong mentally. We grow spiritually by coming to church school and worship, by praying, and by reading the Bible.

All of these things help us to grow strong. God helps us to grow strong, too. In our lives, there may be times that feel stormy. There may be times when we find ourselves in the middle of of problems or sadness. When we are following God, we can feel stronger.

Let's pray—

Dear God, thank you for being in our lives. Be with each one of us. Help us to develop a deep relationship with you. Help us to be strong. Amen.

7
When God Hides

Theme Sometimes it feels like God hides
Scripture Psalm 22
Object Blanket

This story was told the Sunday after one of our church's children died suddenly. Many different emotions and questions were raised during the week. If your congregation ever faces the tragedy of losing a child, I pray that this story might be helpful.

GOOD MORNING! I'M GLAD WE'RE together today. I brought something from my house to show all of you. This is a blanket we keep on our family room couch.

(Adjust this paragraph to describe your own blanket.) We all use this blanket. Grandma Rhodes made it. It is made out of material scraps, and it really feels good. When someone in our family is sick, we usually cover the sick person with this blanket. When we are cold, it makes us feel warm.

Actually, it is not called a blanket. It is called a comforter. This blanket is a comfort to our family.

Do any of you have a special blanket or teddy bear or doll that helps you feel better? Maybe you keep it in bed with you. That special friend is a comfort to you. Have you ever lost this special bear or blanket or doll?

If you have lost it, you feel awful because you want it with you. It helps you feel better. It is a comfort.

Something really sad happened to our church family this week. Our friend Deonte died. We are sad because we won't see Deonte again. Sometimes when we feel really sad, it feels as though God is not with us. It feels as though God is far away. It may even feel as though God has hidden from us.

We learn in church school and worship that God is always with us. Even when it doesn't feel like God is close, we still know that God is there. When we are sad that Deonte died, God feels sad, too.

Try to remember that God is with us. God is with us just like a blanket wrapped around our shoulders or like a teddy bear that we hug. God wants to comfort us.

Let's pray—

Dear God, thank you for being with us even when it feels like you are far away. Thank you, God, for comforting us. We ask you to be with Deonte's family. Amen.

8

The Good Shepherd

Theme Jesus is our guide
Scripture Psalm 23
Object A picture of Jesus with sheep

WELCOME TO OUR TIME together. How many of you know what a shepherd is? What does a shepherd do? *(Encourage the children to share their ideas.)* You have good ideas.

Shepherds have tough jobs. They must protect the sheep in their care. They must protect their sheep from all kinds of trouble: wild animals, swift water, and dangerous wires. Sometimes, shepherds even risk their lives for the sheep.

Sheep are easily scared and need a shepherd to comfort them. The shepherd knows the sheep well. Each shepherd has a special call or tone of voice to use for gathering the sheep. The sheep recognize this call and turn to their leader, the shepherd. Where there are sheep, there will be a shepherd.

Did you know that Jesus is our shepherd? Jesus is called the Good Shepherd. The Good Shepherd never leaves his "sheep." Jesus knows us personally and takes care of us.

We are called to love one another and to love God. When we hear the call of Jesus, we should follow. We follow our leader, our shepherd—Jesus. Jesus cares for us, leads us, and offers us security and safety. Jesus isn't only with us for one day. Jesus is with us every day of our lives. We can trust and follow Jesus.

Let's pray—
Dear God, thanks for guiding us, loving us, and being with us each day. Amen.

9

*T*he Recipe for Our Lives

Theme Our Bible is a treasured book
Scripture Psalm 119:105
Object Cookbook and Bible

*G*OOD MORNING! I HAVE A BOOK I want to show you this morning. Do you know what kind of book this is? *(Show the cookbook.)* What do you use a cookbook for? You are right; you use it to bake and to cook.

In order for food to turn out right, we need to follow the recipes. What if we decide to cook something we have never cooked before? What if we choose not to follow a recipe? How would the food turn out? It might be a big mess.

There is another book that also gives us instructions. *(Show the Bible.)* The Bible gives us the recipe for our lives. It has rules called the Ten Commandments. It has instructions on how we should pray.

The Bible has not only instructions but also many other wonderful things. There are words that comfort us. There are stories from long ago: stories about a beautiful queen; a man named Jonah and a big fish; a man named Noah, his ark, and the animals; a giant, a little boy, and a slingshot. There are stories about Jesus' birth and stories Jesus told as he walked from place to place with his friends.

There is even a place in the Bible where Jesus talks about how children are special. It says:

Then little children were being brought to him in order that he might lay his hands on them and pray. The disciples spoke sternly to those who brought them but Jesus said, "Let the little children come to me, and do not stop them; for it is to such as these that the kingdom of heaven belongs." And he laid his hands on them and went on his way. Matthew 19:13-15

Remember that the Bible is a special book. It is a collection of words that makes us feel better, a collection of ideas to remember, and a collection of wonderful stories.

Let's pray—

Dear God, thank you for the Bible. Thank you for the wonderful stories, words of comfort, and ideas to remember. We are thankful that we are all special to you. Amen.

10

A Sampling of Proverbs

Theme Samples of proverbs regarding our words
Scripture Proverbs
Object The Bible

I'M HAPPY YOU CAME TO WORSHIP this morning. You know our Bible has wonderful stories. There are wonderful words and treasures inside these pages.

Some people call our Bible a library because there are many books inside these covers. One of those books is called Proverbs. In the book of Proverbs are many sayings and statements that give us ideas for how we should live. These ideas are sometimes called words of wisdom because they are values that God wants us to have in our lives.

I wanted to share some of these proverbs and wise sayings with you, but I ran into a problem. I discovered that all of the proverbs were written for adults. They were written to be understood by grown-ups.

So I decided to pick a few of these proverbs and change them just a bit, so that they are easier for you to understand. Listen to these proverbs:

Care and worries make us feel sad, but happy words help us feel better (Prov. 12:25).

People who don't care about God's words bring trouble to themselves. People who do care about God's words will be rewarded (Prov. 13:13).

A kind word can calm anger, but a mean word will stir anger (Prov. 15:1).

A right word is like a treasure (Prov. 25:11).

The words from God are true; the words from God are a comfort to us. (Prov. 30:5).

All of these proverbs remind us that our words are important. We need to use our words carefully. When we use our words carefully and share words that God gives us, we can help other people.

Let's pray—

Dear God, thank you for all the words you share with us in the Bible. Help us to use our words wisely so that we may be kind and helpful to others. Amen.

11
Known by God

Theme God knows us before we are born
Scripture Jeremiah 1:4-10
Object Baby book

GOOD MORNING! IT'S A JOY to see all of you. Today, I brought along a baby book. Have you seen a book like this before? Most moms and dads have these books.

This is Erica's book, and I got her permission to bring it. A baby book is a collection of memories of your birth and early childhood. Your mom and dad might have saved pictures and cards to remember your birth. They might have kept a list of who came to visit or of the gifts that you received. Perhaps, they recorded special dates such as your first tooth or your first word.

Do you know that God doesn't need a book like this to remember special things about you? God knows each one of us very well.

Once when God was talking to Jeremiah, God said, "I knew you before you were formed and before you were born, I blessed you." This means that God knew Jeremiah for a long time, even before Jeremiah was born. God gave a blessing to Jeremiah.

God's words to Jeremiah have a special meaning for us, too. God is with us each day of our lives. When we need to do something new, God is with us. When we are frightened, God is with us. God knows each of us, God loves each of us, and God has blessed each of us.

It doesn't matter whether you are three, seven, fourteen, or ninety-nine; God knows you, loves you, and blesses you!

Let's pray—

Dear God, we are glad you know us and love us. Thank you for blessing us. Thank you for being with us each day. Amen.

12

*P*rayer—Anytime, Anywhere

Theme We can pray anytime, anywhere, about anything
Scripture Jeremiah 33:3
Object Three pipe cleaners

Practice ahead of time. Fold the three pipe cleaners into one "stick person." Bend one pipe cleaner into a loop for the head with the ends of the pipe cleaner remaining straight. Attach another pipe cleaner for arms. Add the last pipe cleaner for legs. Adjust the pipe cleaners to make the stick figure. Then bend the pipe cleaners into the positions mentioned.

TODAY IN OUR WORSHIP, we want to think about prayer. Prayer is talking and listening to God. As we think together about prayer, I'm going to fold these pipe cleaners into different body shapes. Watch and listen.

We can pray to God anytime, anywhere, and about anything.

Some people pray on their knees.

Some people pray with their hands folded.

Some people pray with their heads bowed.

Some people pray with their eyes closed.

It doesn't matter in what position we pray. God always listens.

Sometimes, we pray by ourselves.

Sometimes, we pray as a group.

Sometimes, we pray aloud.

Sometimes, we pray silently and only God hears us.

It doesn't matter how we pray. God always listens.

We can pray at mealtime.

We can pray at bedtime.

We can pray at other times of the day.

We can pray when we are troubled or when we are thankful.

It doesn't matter when we pray. God always listens and wants to hear our prayers, whether they are thankful and joyful or troubled and sad. Remember that you can pray anytime, anywhere, and about anything.

Let's pray—

Dear God, what a wonderful gift we have in prayer. Thank you for always listening to us no matter when, where, or how we pray. Amen.

13

*W*hat Does God Ask?

Theme How should we follow God?
Scripture Micah 6:8
Object Shapes of hand, heart, and foot cut from paper

WELCOME! I want to show you somethin. What is this shape? It is a hand; you are correct. I traced around Joel's hand and cut it out of the paper.

We do many things with our hands. Let's name a few. (*Encourage lots of responses.*) There are many things we can do with our hands. We take care of ourselves. We use our hands to do our work. We use our hands to care for one another and show kindness.

We can help others when they are sad or scared. We can pat them on the back. We can shake hands. We can give them a gift of some sort. We use our hands to show kindness.

I want to show you something else. What is this shape? It is a heart; you are correct. A heart shape is a symbol of what? (*Encourage them to say "love."*) Yes, a heart shape is a symbol of love. We love one another. We know that God tells us to love one another. God wants us to love people and to show them our love. Our hands and our hearts work together to show love and kindness to other people.

I have one more shape to show you. What is this shape? It is a foot; you are right. Sometimes we talk about walking with God. That is another way of saying we are trying to live the way God wants us to live. We try to obey what God asks of us. We know that God asks us to do what is right. We need to try to do what is kind and fair.

One verse in the Bible says, "Do justice, love kindness, and walk humbly with your God." That means God asks us to be fair, to be loving and kind, and to obey what God teaches us. We use our hands, our hearts, and our feet as we follow God by being fair, loving, and kind.

Let's pray—

Dear God, each day please help us to follow you. Help us to show your love by what we do. May our hands, our hearts, and our feet serve you. Amen.

14
*N*amed by God

Theme We are God's children
Scripture Matthew 3:13-17
Object None

This story invites you to say the children's names to remind them that they are loved by God. You might want to review their names ahead of time. If you forget a name, don't be embarrassed to ask the child.

*T*HIS MORNING I NEED your help with the story. Listen carefully so you know when to help. How many of you have ridden in a boat on a river?

Sometimes, we ride on the water. Sometimes, we travel over the water on bridges. Wriggle your fingers slowly and imagine a river that is flowing peacefully.

Now wriggle your fingers faster. Imagine a river that is flowing quickly. The way a river flows depends on the weather and the amount of water in the river.

I want to tell you a Bible story about a river. A man named John the Baptist was standing near a river. Imagine a gently flowing river, a quiet river.

John was preaching to the people. He encouraged them to change their lives, to follow God, and to live the way God wanted them to live. He told the people to be baptized to show they had changed and were following God.

Many people decided to be baptized. While John was baptizing the people, Jesus came to the river. Jesus asked John to baptize him. John said, "But, Jesus, you are the Son of God. I should be baptized by you."

Jesus said this was the right thing to do, so John agreed and baptized Jesus. After Jesus was baptized, the Spirit of God came down from heaven like a dove. A voice from heaven said, "This is my Son. I love him."

Do you know that God loves you, too? Each one of you (*say each child's name*) is God's child and God loves you.

Let's pray—

Thanks, God, for your great love for us. Thank you for calling each one of us your child. Amen.

15

*P*eople Gathered to Hear Jesus Preach

Theme Jesus teaches us many things
Scripture Matthew 5-7
Object Picture of Jesus teaching

WHEN JESUS WAS ON EARTH, he taught in many places. He taught from a boat, along a roadside, on a mountain, and wherever people gathered to hear him. Many people came to hear what Jesus said.

People believed Jesus could heal their illnesses and problems if they were near him. Some people tried to touch the hem of his robe. Some asked him to make them well.

One day when Jesus saw the crowd of people gathered to hear him teach, he climbed up a mountain. He started talking to his disciples, but the other people could hear him teaching as well.

The words Jesus said are usually called "The Sermon on the Mount," but this wasn't like the sermons we hear now. This sermon lasted for several days. People probably came and went. People probably brought picnic lunches. And perhaps the children played together on the hillside.

The people listened carefully. Jesus told them how to be happy and enjoy God's blessings. Jesus told the people to be kind, to be peaceful, and to do what was right. This message from Jesus was so important that it is included in our Bible.

I like to think that Jesus taught in a caring manner. He wanted the people to hear his good news. I also think that Jesus held out his hands to the people to welcome them.

Jesus wants to welcome us, too. Jesus wants us to listen, learn, and know we are loved.

Let's pray—
Dear God, thank you for the wonderful teachings of Jesus. Help us to be happy and enjoy the blessings in our lives. Amen.

16
A Joyful Time

Theme There is joy in being a Christian
Scripture Matthew 11:28-30
Object Collage of pictures of things that make us happy

Ahead of time, search through magazines for pictures of things that make us happy. Create a collage or show the pictures individually.

ARE ALL OF YOU HAPPY? I see smiles. That's good! I would like to show you a poster that Joel and I made. On this poster, we put pictures of things that make us happy. What are they?

(*Describe your own photos.*) 1) Playing outside in the leaves, 2) playhouses in the snow, 3) our cat, 4) getting a letter in the mail, 5) playing with Play-Doh, 6) sunshine, 7) family members, and 8) pumpkins.

Are there other things that make you happy? (*Let the children share their ideas.*) There are lots of things that make you happy!

There is something that all of us have in our lives that can make us happy. That is God! We can be happy that God is with us and invites us into the kingdom. Being a Christian is something to be joyful about! It is good to be in God's kingdom.

Sometimes, it may be difficult to follow God. Maybe a friend wants you to do something you know you shouldn't do. You may have a difficult decision to make. Remember, following God is the right thing to do, and having God in our lives makes us happy! Think of all the things in your life that make you happy: your family, your pets, your toys—and don't forget about God!

Let's pray—
Dear God, thank you for all the special things in our lives. Thank you for the invitation to be part of your kingdom. Amen.

17

Seventy Times Seven

Theme Forgiveness is great
Scripture Matthew 18:21-35
Object Jar with seven M&Ms and jar with 490 M&Ms

*L*ET'S TALK ABOUT THE NUMBER seven. First, we will count seven children. *(Count seven children.)* Second, let's have seven choir members stand. *(Alert the choir director to this before the worship service.)* Third, I would like to show you seven M&Ms in this small jar.

In our Scripture today, we hear Jesus telling us to forgive seventy times seven. Jesus and his friend Peter are having a discussion about forgiveness. Peter wants to know how many times he should forgive another person. Jesus tells Peter, "Do not only forgive seven times, but forgive seventy times seven."

Do you know that 70 x 7 is a lot compared to 7? 70 x 7 equals 490. Let's compare this jar of seven M&Ms to this jar of 490 M&Ms. Do you see a great difference?

Jesus was using these numbers as an example. He was teaching us that forgiveness cannot be measured. We should forgive freely. Forgiveness should be without limits. When we ask for forgiveness, God forgives us. Forgiveness is a gift. We can give that gift to others.

Sometimes forgiving is not easy, but it is very important. God freely forgives us, and we should forgive other people, too.

Let's pray—

Dear God, thank you for the forgiveness you give us. We are grateful for your kindness. Help us to forgive other people, too. Sometimes forgiving a person who has hurt us is difficult. Help us to be forgiving. Amen.

18

*H*earts and Hands United

Theme Jesus asks us to serve others
Scripture Matthew 25:34-40
Object A service project

This story has a place to introduce a service project. Either the children or the entire church family could participate in such a project. Your denominational or local leaders may have suggestions for projects.

WELCOME TO OUR SPECIAL TIME during the worship service. We are fortunate to have many blessings. We can use our senses to enjoy the beauty of the world God created. We have the blessing of knowing God is with us always. Many of us have plenty of food and clothes. We can get help when we are sick or need care in some way.

Not all people are so fortunate. Some people in our community, country, or world struggle each day for basic needs in their lives. There are many reasons why people struggle. Sometimes, the ground they use for farming is not good, and their crops do not grow well. Sometimes, a weather disaster such as a hurricane or flood hits a country and causes many problems. Sometimes, a whole area is poor because there aren't enough ways to earn money. Sometimes, there aren't enough doctors and nurses to help keep people well. People struggle for different reasons.

Jesus asks us to serve others. He served others when he helped the sick and talked to the lonely. He served his disciples by humbly getting on his knees to his knees to wash their feet. Jesus showed us how to serve.

Jesus told us in Scripture that when we help others, it is as though we are helping Jesus himself. When we give food or drink or clothes or company to someone in need, we are serving Jesus. Watch and listen for times when you can help people who have need.

(Introduce your particular service project. Don't make this too long or you will lose the children's interest. Be prepared with information to send home to each family, explaining how each child can participate.)

Let's pray—

Dear God, thank you for the many blessings we have. You are the giver of many gifts. Help us to see where we can help other people. Help us to serve you with our hearts and our hands. Amen.

19
Time with the Children

Theme Children are loved
Scripture Mark 10:13-16
Object Worship bulletin, picture of Jesus with children

WELCOME TO OUR TIME TOGETHER. Today I would like to show you something in our worship bulletin. What does this say? *(Point to the phrase "time with the children" or the appropriate phrase in your bulletin.)*

We consider this part of our worship service to be important. Each one of you is important to our church. We love you and care for you. Each of you has a special place in the family of God. We want to share God's good news with you. That is why we have a special time for you during our worship.

I would like to show you something else. This is a picture of Jesus with a group of children. Do you see how all the children are gathered close to Jesus? Jesus wanted children close to him.

His disciples were protective of Jesus, and they told the people to take their children away from Jesus. Jesus said, "No! Let the little children come to me. Don't stop them for they belong to the kingdom."

Jesus took the children in his arms and blessed them. Jesus loved all of the children who had gathered around him, and Jesus also loves each of you.

This morning we want you to know that you are loved by your church family. We want you to know that you are loved by Jesus, and that his love never stops!

Let's pray—

Dear Jesus, thanks for your great love for us. We are glad that you love all people. Amen.

20

Love One Another

Theme Share God's love
Scripture Mark 12:28-34
Object Paper and envelope for each child

GOOD MORNING! I'm so pleased that you came to our service of worship this morning. One of God's great gifts to us is his wonderful love. That love never ends. That love doesn't stop even when we do something we shouldn't do.

God's love is with us all the time. Some people compare God's love to things in our world. For example, people might say God's love is greater than the tallest mountain or the deepest ocean. The most important thing to remember is that God loves each of us very much.

Other important gifts God gives us are the soul and mind and strength to love God and to love other people. God wants us to share love with other people. When we love other people, we are sharing God's great love.

In the Bible, Jesus says, "Love the Lord your God with all your heart, with all your soul, with all your mind, and with all your strength." Jesus also teaches, "Love your neighbor as your self."

When we love God and love the people around us, we are obeying the commandments God gives us. I want you to think about how to obey God's commandment to love our neighbors as we love ourselves.

To help you with that challenge, I have a piece of paper and an envelope for each of you. I want you to think of someone with whom you can share God's love.

Write a letter to that person. Or draw a picture for them. Ask your parents to help you if you can't think of what to say or what to draw. Use the envelope to mail the letter. By doing this, you will be sharing your love and God's love.

Let's pray—

Dear God, we are glad for your great love. Thanks for your love that never stops. Help us to share this great love with other people. Amen.

21

*A*nswer the Call

Theme Answer the call to share God's love
Scripture Luke 5:1-11
Object Hearts for each child

*H*ELLO THIS MORNING! I'm glad to see all of you. When Jesus was on earth teaching and preaching, he decided to find some helpers. Jesus knew he could teach these helpers, and they, too, could teach other people.

One day Jesus was walking along the Sea of Galilee. He saw some men who were fishing. They weren't fishing like you might see people fishing. They weren't using fishing poles and bait. They were using large rope nets that they threw into the water. Then they would pull the nets out and hope they were full of fish.

Jesus called to the fishermen, saying, "Come, follow me, and I will make you fish for people." Do you think Jesus meant for them to throw their nets around the people? No.

The fishermen probably didn't know exactly what Jesus meant, but they knew the right thing to do was to follow Jesus. They heard Jesus talk about God's love. They learned how wonderful God's love was.

They learned that when Jesus said they would fish for people, he meant they would share God's wonderful love with other people. He meant they would share the good news. Jesus also asks each one of us to share this wonderful love and good news.

I have something for each of you. I have a heart cut from a piece of construction paper. Share this heart with someone sometime this week. When you share your paper heart, remember you will be sharing God's love.

Let's pray—

Dear God, thank you for your great love. Help us to pass this love on to other people. Amen.

22

*T*he Gift of Prayer

Theme Jesus taught his disciples and us how to pray
Scripture Luke 11:1-13
Object Prayer card showing the Lord's Prayer

*I*HAVE A QUESTION FOR YOU. Have you ever had a hard time getting your mom's or your dad's attention? Have you ever wanted to ask them a question or tell them something when it seemed like they just plain weren't listening?

That happens sometimes. Grown-ups don't mean for it to happen, but sometimes we're thinking of many things. We have a hard time listening. How do you get your mom's or dad's attention?

Do you know that God is always ready to listen when we pray? We never need to work at getting God's attention.

When Jesus and his special friends, the disciples, were together, the disciples asked Jesus to teach them how to pray. They asked Jesus to help them know what words to say when they talked to God.

Jesus taught the disciples how to pray. In his teaching, Jesus also taught us how to pray. The prayer Jesus used when he was teaching is called the Lord's Prayer.

In this prayer we can—

Pray to Our Father in Heaven and know that God is hearing us.

Promise that we are respecting and loving God.

Tell God we believe God knows what is best for us.

Know that God gives us all we need and more: things like food, houses, and people to care for us.

Accept God's forgiveness and forgive others.

Ask God for guidance and help.

Tell God that we think God is great.

I have a little prayer card for each one of you. *(Go to last pages of the book for text of a sample prayer card I developed for each child.)* Maybe you know this prayer already. If you don't, ask someone to help you learn it. This is a prayer you can use all of your life.

Let's pray—

Dear God, we are glad you listen to our prayers. Thank you for being great. Amen.

23

Be a Welcomer

Theme Jesus wants us to show hospitality
Scripture Luke 14:7-14
Object Smile stickers

*A*ND HELLO AGAIN. I'm glad to see all of you! Usually when I give you something during our story time, I give it to you after the prayer. Today, I'm going to give you something at the beginning of our time.

I have a smile sticker for each one of you. How about taking one and putting it on your shirt? You look great with that smiling face sticker! And, you always look great with that wonderful smile that God gave to you.

Our smiles are all different. Some of you are missing some teeth, and you have holes in your smile. But the missing teeth don't make your smiles any less beautiful.

How do you feel when someone smiles at you? Right; you feel good, you feel special, you feel like someone likes you, you feel happy.

It is important for us to smile. When you smile at someone, they feel like they are important to you. They feel that you think they are special.

Sometimes it's easy to smile. You smile at the people you know, the people you like, the people who make you laugh. Do you know some people really need smiles?

Think about someone you may not like very well. Maybe that person has been unkind to you or maybe they dress differently from the way you dress. Each of us may have someone we know whom we find difficult to like. Do you know it is especially important to give them a smile?

Jesus tells us to be kind to people who are different. Jesus wants us to smile and be kind to people who have problems, to people who are poor, and to people who are sick. A smile is like a welcome sign for people to feel good.

When we are kind to people, we are sharing the wonderful love of Jesus with them.

Let's pray—

Dear God, help us to be kind to all people, even people we may not like very much. Help us to smile and show love to them. Amen.

24

*P*ut on Your Jesus Glasses

Theme We need to see our world as Jesus does
Scripture Luke 16:19-31
Object Variety of eyeglasses (reading glasses, sun-
glasses, protective glasses, swimming goggles, etc.)

*I*AM ALWAYS SO GLAD TO SEE each one of you. Our
church family is happy you are with us! Let's see—
do we have anyone here this morning who wears
glasses? *(Check your group to see if anyone wears glasses.
Be prepared for no one to have glasses! Be sure you have
some sample glasses with you.)*

How does wearing a pair of glasses help you? Yes,
they help you to see better. Many of us develop weak-
nesses in our eyes, and we need glasses to help us see
better.

(Adapt this paragraph for your example.) I started
wearing glasses when I was about your age. I needed
to wear my glasses all of the time. When I was a little
older, I got a pair of contact lenses to help me see. But I
still have a pair of glasses. I always need extra help to
be able to see well.

There are other kinds of glasses. *(Hold up glasses as
you describe them.)* We call these glasses sunglasses.
People wear them when the sun is shining brightly.

We call these glasses protective glasses. People
wear glasses like these to protect their eyes when

they're working with something that could hurt their eyes.

These glasses are ones we call swimming goggles. Swimmers wear these goggles so they can open their eyes when swimming under water.

It is important for us to see well. It is also important for us to see the things that Jesus wants us to see. For example, Jesus taught his disciples to help people who needed care.

We can see when someone else is unhappy, and we can help that person. Maybe there are times in your family when you will see that someone is extra tired. Maybe you can help them in some way. Trying to see as Jesus sees is like putting on a pair of "Jesus glasses." By seeing as Jesus sees and helping one another, we are sharing the great love of Jesus.

So each day pretend you are putting on a pair of Jesus glasses. See where you can help someone else.

Let's pray—

Dear God, you help each one of us in so many ways. Help us to see how we can help each other, too. Amen.

25

*T*he Arrival of the King
Palm Sunday

Theme We remember the king
Scripture Mark 11:1-11
Object An emerald palm

Emerald palms are available at many florist shops.

TODAY IS PALM SUNDAY—a special day! We remember Jesus entering Jerusalem on a donkey. Thfe people were excited to see Jesus. They waved palm branches. They laid their branches and coats on the road for Jesus to ride on as he went through the town.

The people said, "Hosanna! Blessed is he who comes in the name of the Lord." The people knew they were seeing a king. They knew Jesus was special. We remember this special day by waving palm branches and singing.

I would like to show you a particular type of palm. I learned this week that this type of palm is called an emerald palm. It is a symbol of kingship.

Do you see the many sections of the palm? It has many points. These remind us of a crown. The palms can be separated so that each person can have one. Each person, every single one of us, is very special to to Jesus.

We can also wave the palms to remind us that we are a community. We are a group of people who love Jesus.

The pieces of the palm can either be waved separately or together. We are all important members in God's kingdom. Each of us is special, but we can also work together for good in the kingdom of God.

By our words and actions, we can show other people that Jesus is the king of our lives. We show that Jesus is the king of our lives by loving the people of the world and by doing the things that Jesus wants us to do.

The palms remind us of the great love Jesus had for us. The palms remind us, too, that we can all work together to tell others about how special it is to have Jesus in our lives.

Let's pray—

Dear God, by waving our palms we remember the day Jesus came to Jerusalem. We remember that Jesus is a king whom we love. We thank you that Jesus loves us. Amen.

26

A Time of Service
Maundy Thursday

Theme Jesus served his disciples by washing their feet
Scripture John 13:1-20
Object Towel and basin

WE ARE IN A SPECIAL WEEK. We call this "Holy Week." Do you remember that last Sunday we talked about Jesus coming to Jerusalem? The people knew Jesus was special. They wanted to honor Jesus. As Jesus rode into the city on a donkey, the people celebrated his arrival by waving palm branches and laying their coats on the ground.

Many things happened to Jesus during that week. He went to a special gathering with his disciples, his friends. They had a meal together.

Jesus knew he would soon leave his friends to return to his father in heaven. He knew he would soon die. So before he left his friends, he did something very special.

He took a towel and a basin. *(Show these items reverently to the children. You may even want to pour water into the basin.)* Jesus poured water into the basin and knelt to wash each of his disciples' feet. This was a very special event.

In Jesus' time, it was hospitality, which means kindness, to offer guests water to wash their feet. The people often wore sandals and walked along dusty roads. The washing of feet was refreshing. Washing a guest's feet was an act of service.

For Jesus to wash the feet of the disciples was a special event. The disciples sensed the importance of this evening together with Jesus. By washing the feet of his friends, Jesus showed us how to be servants. Jesus showed us one way to offer love to one another.

Jesus asks us to find ways in our lives to serve one another. We can follow the example of Jesus and show love to the people in our lives.

Let's pray—

Dear Jesus, we know it was a special time for you with the disciples. Thank you for showing us how to be servants. Help us to find ways to show love to other people. Amen.

27

A Dark Day
Good Friday

Theme Jesus suffered greatly
Scripture John 19:1-30
Object Cross draped in black

*T*ODAY WE ARE REMEMBERING a sad day. This day is called "Good Friday." We sometimes wonder why it is called Good Friday when something so awful happened.

Our cross is draped with a black cloth because we remember this is the day Jesus died on the cross. We remember a difficult word. That word is *crucifixion.* Crucifixion means Jesus died by being hung on a cross.

Jesus was treated very badly. The people who didn't like him did cruel things to him. They beat him. The soldiers made a crown of thorns and placed it on his head. Do you know what thorns are?

Have you ever been walking in the woods when you got caught by a bush that had prickly things on it? Those prickly things are often called thorns. Can you imagine a circle of thorns on your head?

The people put the crown of thorns on Jesus because they were making fun of him and calling him "King of the Jews." The soldiers took Jesus to a hill outside the town. They made Jesus carry his own cross. When they got to the hill, which was called "the Place of the Skull," the soldiers nailed Jesus to the cross. They were so mean to Jesus that they even took his clothes.

Jesus' family and friends were gathered near the cross. The pain they felt at the crucifixion of Jesus was great. They were losing someone they loved dearly.

Jesus asked his good friend John to care for his mother. When Jesus knew he would soon die, he said, "It is finished." He bowed his head and gave up his spirit.

Jesus' friends asked for his body. They wanted to be sure it was cared for properly. They wrapped the body with strips of linen and spices. They carefully laid his body in a tomb in a nearby garden.

This is a very sad story. We feel sad because Jesus, whom we love so much, was hurt in this painful way. We feel sorry when the people we love suffer.

On this day, we remember the great sacrifice Jesus made for us—the sacrifice of his life. We know, however, that the story doesn't end with Jesus in the tomb. We will hear the good news part of the story on Sunday morning.

Let's pray—

O God, you must have suffered, too, on the day your son died. We remember the great sacrifice Jesus made for us. He gave his life for us. Amen.

28

A Surprising Moment
Easter

Theme The empty tomb was a great surprise
Scripture Luke 24:1-12
Object Large egg shape filled with confetti

*Do you need to get someone's permission before you use con-
fetti during the worship service? You can find Easter confetti at many party stores.*

*H*APPY EASTER! What a great day this is when we
celebrate the good news that Jesus lives! Did all
of you have an Easter basket this morning? Did you
get some eggs in your basket?

Getting Easter eggs is fun. The eggs are not only
good to eat, but they remind us of new life. We have
new life because Jesus lives!

I have an egg with me that I would like to show all
of you. It is not quite as pretty or as colorful as a dyed
egg. But, it is a special egg.

*(Before the story time, tell your "egg opener" the egg is
filled with colorful Easter confetti. Encourage the egg opener
to fling the confetti over the children to create a mood of joyful surprise!)* Would you like to open this egg for us?

That egg was full of Easter confetti! What a surprise! Confetti is used at times of celebration. Easter is
certainly a time to celebrate.

A long time ago on the first Easter morning, some friends of Jesus went to the tomb where his body had been placed. They went to the tomb sadly because their dear friend and leader was gone.

Their sadness turned to confusion when they realized that the body of Jesus was gone. Their confusion turned to joyful surprise when Jesus appeared before them, and they realized he was alive.

Each Easter morning we celebrate with joy that Jesus is alive. What wonderful, joyful, good news we have to share because Jesus lives! That wonderful good news makes us want to celebrate.

Now what shall we do about this confetti? First, I have a bag of confetti for each one of you. After our prayer, I will give the bags to you. But please wait until you get home to open them.

Second, after our worship service is finished, please come back here. If you help us pick up this confetti from the floor, you can keep that, too.

Let's pray—

Dear God, what a joyful surprise it was that first Easter morning when Jesus' friends learned he was alive. Thank you for this good news that we still celebrate. Amen.

29
*H*ard to Believe

Theme The disciples had a difficult time believing Jesus was the risen Lord
Scripture Luke 24:38-46
Object One cocoon; paper butterflies for everyone

Search for a cocoon for this story. The concept is this: it is hard to believe a butterfly will emerge from something that appears dry and hard. If you cannot find a cocoon, substitute a flower bud or apple seed. Adjust the story accordingly, describing changes these items experience as they evolve. Emphasize that we all have a difficult time imagining how things change.

I WANT TO SHOW YOU SOMETHING this morning. I brought a cocoon with me for our time together. It looks hard, dry, and brown. I'm sure that at least some of you know what comes out of a cocoon.

What comes from a cocoon? A butterfly comes out! You're right! It is hard to believe that a beautiful butterfly comes out of a dry, hard cocoon. It is one of those interesting things about nature.

Once time the disciples saw Jesus and had a hard time believing it was was Jesus. They knew Jesus had died. When Jesus appeared, they were scared. They were filled with fear. They had not expected to see Jesus. But Jesus said, "Don't be frightened. Touch my hands. Touch my feet. It is really me."

When the disciples believed it was really Jesus, he told them they had important jobs to do. Jesus told the disciples they were witnesses and should share the story of Jesus with other people.

For the rest of their lives, the disciples tried to do what Jesus told them to do. They traveled many places to tell many people about the good news.

I have something for you. I have a little paper butterfly to tape on your shirt or dress. We know that butterflies are signs of new life.

We each have new life because of Jesus. Because we have new life in Jesus, we can be like the disciples and help other people believe in Jesus, too.

Let's pray—

Dear God, thank you for the new life we have. Help us to share with other people so they, too, may believe. Amen.

30
*E*aster People

Theme Let us take Easter joy with us everyday
Scripture John 20:19-31
Object Small crosses

*G*OOD MORNING! I'm glad to see all of you! This is the first Sunday after Easter. Easter is such an exciting time. We remember the good news that Jesus lives. We are joyful because Jesus is with us.

Guess what? Easter lasts for more than one day. Easter is a season that lasts for several weeks in the church year. Easter can also be a feeling, a joyful feeling.

We are Easter people because we believe in the good news that Jesus lives. We can let that good news be an important part of our lives. We can keep Easter joy with us each day. We know that Jesus loves us very much. That gives us joy, too.

As you grow up, you will discover your special talents. You can use your talents to serve the church. You can also keep Easter joy with you as you serve the church.

After our prayer, I will give you something to help you remember to keep Easter joy with you everyday. I have small crosses for each of you.

When Jesus died, the cross was a symbol of sadness. We know that sadness turned to joy when Jesus was resurrected. When we know that Jesus lives with each one of us, the cross means love, hope, and for-giveness. May this cross remind you to keep Easter joy!

Let's pray—
Dear God, thank you for the joy that following Jesus gives to us. Help us to be joyful, faithful follow-ers. Amen.

31

A Time to Rejoice

Theme Share the joy of the risen Jesus
Scripture 1 Peter 1:3-9
Object Smile stickers; the letters J O Y

WELCOME TO OUR STORY TIME! I have some simple questions for you. Who knows what letter this is? That's right; this is a "J." How about this one? That's right; this is an "O." And what is this? That's right; this is a "Y."

If we put these letters together, what word do they spell? You are exactly right—JOY. Who knows what joy is? *(Encourage answers.)* Yes, joy is a feeling like happiness. Can you think of a time you were really happy?

There are many times in our lives when we are joyful. We have joy in our families. We have joy when we see the beautiful things in nature. We have joy with friends. We also have joy because we know that Jesus lives with each one of us. *(Adjust the next sentence if this story does not follow Easter Sunday.)* We were all joyful last week because it was Easter. We are joyful because we know that Jesus is alive!

We call one Sunday during the year Easter Sunday. But that doesn't mean that our joy about Jesus being alive should last only for that day. Our Easter joy should be with us every day because Jesus is alive. That is really joyful news!

Each one of you has a great smile. A smile shows joy. I have some smile stickers with me. Because there are several stickers, what do you think I am going to ask you to do? *(Wait for their answers and encourage them.)* You're right! Share some of these stickers with other people, and remind them to be joyful. Remind them to have Easter joy.

Let's pray—

Dear God, it is great to have joy in our lives. Help us to remember that Easter joy can last everyday. Amen.

32
Go into the World

Theme Go into the world with God's good news
Scripture Luke 24:44-53
Object Paper cut in shapes of a person and of a cloud

*H*ELLO AGAIN! I'M GLAD all of you are here this morning. Do you remember several weeks ago when we celebrated Easter? We were glad that Jesus was alive.

Today, we remember another important time for Jesus and his disciples. After Jesus arose from the dead, he was with his special friends, the disciples, for a short time. During this short time, he talked with them.

Jesus taught the disciples some important things, and all of them learned together. This time together was important for both Jesus and his disciples.

One day, Jesus told his disciples to gather on a hillside. Jesus gave them a special job to do. Jesus said, "Go into all the world and tell everyone the good news of God. Tell everyone that God loves them."

(Be prepared with your two pieces of paper. Hold the cloud shape in one hand and the shape of the person to illustrate Jesus in the other hand. Slowly demonstrate Jesus ascending to the cloud.) Then something very mysterious happened. Grown-ups even have a hard time understanding this. Jesus began to rise up, and he disap-

peared into the clouds. He was returning to God his father.

The disciples were amazed at what they saw. They began to praise God and continued with the special work that Jesus had asked them to do. They went into all the world sharing God's good news.

Each one of us is a disciple of Jesus. We can share God's good news, too. Do you know that each of you has special talents given to you by God? As you grow and as you develop those special talents, you can share God's good news.

Each day, there will be ways for you to share the good news. When you are a good sport in a ball game, you are sharing God's love. When you help another person, you are sharing God's love. Try to find at least one way each day to share God's good news.

Let's pray—

Dear God, thank you for the things Jesus taught the disciples. Thank you for teaching us. Help us to be good disciples, too. Amen.

33
A *Promise* *Kept*

Theme Jesus keeps his promises
Scripture John 14:15-21
Object None

*U*SUALLY I BRING SOMETHING TO show you during our time together. Today, I want to talk about something you cannot see. It is something very real, but you just can't see it.

The thing I am talking about is a promise. Most of you have heard the word "promise" before. Can you give me an example of a promise? *(Welcome their responses.)*

Even though you can't see promises, you can see symbols of promises. A handshake is a promise. A wedding ring is a symbol of a promise. Have you seen your parents write a check? A check is a symbol of a promise that they are paying for something.

When we make a promise, we need to do everything we can to keep that promise. We need to do our best not to break the promise. When someone makes a promise to us, we need to trust that person. We trust that person to try very hard to keep that promise.

The Bible has promises in its pages. In the story of Noah and the ark, a rainbow became a sign of God's promise. The birth of Jesus is a promise. Jesus promises us that the Holy Spirit will be with us always.

We cannot see the Holy Spirit, so this is a little hard to understand. But Jesus promises us that the Holy Spirit is with us everyday. Even though we cannot see this promise, we know that it is true because Jesus said it. That's a promise we can trust in.

Let's pray—
Dear God, thank you for promises and people we trust. Thank you especially for the promise of the Holy Spirit in our lives. Amen.

34
Special People
Mother's Day

Theme God made each of us special
Scripture Isaiah 66:13
Object Box of dryer sheets, cake mixes, car keys, Bible

*Talking with the children on Mother's or Father's Day—see
next story—can present a challenge because many children
do not live in an intact nuclear family. Remind children that
other adults in their lives can function as mother or father
role models. And God is like a parent to us.*

TODAY IS A SPECIAL DAY. What are we celebrating
today? Mother's Day! This is a day when we remember all the good things moms do for us. We remember to say thank you.

I have some things with me to help you remember
all the good things that moms do. *(Talk about the jobs
mothers do. Use the suggested items or add items of your
own.)*

God helps mothers to be the special people so many
of them are. God guides mothers as they guide their
children. God shares love with mothers so they can
share love with their children.

Sometimes, a grandmother or an aunt or special
friends are also like mothers to us. We are fortunate to
have these special people in our lives.

God helps each of you to be a special person, too. God gives each of us a heart of love, hands to help, and eyes to see God in other people. We remember that God has made each one of us.

Sometimes in school and other places, we want to be like somebody else. We admire their clothes or the things they do, and we want to be like them rather than like ourselves. We need to remember that we are special just the way God made us.

Today, let us thank God for our mothers and for other people who are special to us. Let us also thank God for making each one of us special.

Let's pray—

Dear God, thank you for our mothers who are very special to us. Thank you for other people who are special to us. And thank you for making each one of us special, too. Guide us, God, to follow you. Amen.

35

God Created Fathers
Father's Day

Theme God is a father, guiding, protecting, loving us
Scripture Matthew 6:9
Object Father's Day card

Presenting a story for Father's Day is a special challenge for Christian educators. Many children in our church settings do not have fathers living with them on a daily basis. Be sure to mention in the story that there may be other males who serve as father figures. The best gift of all is having God as a parent.

*D*ID ANY OF YOU SAY "Happy Father's Day" to someone special today? Let me show you this Father's Day card. *(Read the message.)*

This is the day to say thank you to your dad or someone else who may be like a dad to you. Maybe your grandfather or an uncle or a special friend is like a father to you.

What makes fathers special? *(Encourage their responses. Add a few of your own if needed.)* Fathers are special when they talk with and listen to their children. Fathers are special when they play games and have fun. Fathers are special when they have nice smiles that encourage other people. Fathers are special when they give hugs or help their children with problems.

Fathers are special when they help with homework and read stories. Fathers are special when they provide for their families with food and a house. God did a good job when fathers were created.

Do you remember that Jesus called God "Father"? In fact, God is called father in the Bible many times. That doesn't necessarily mean God is a man.

Rather, God is a perfect parent. God leads us and helps us. God listens to us. God helps us when we are sad. God is happy when we are happy. God loves us no matter what. God's love never ends.

We are thankful for our parents, our mom and dad. We are also thankful for our heavenly parent, God, whose love never ends.

Let's pray—

Dear God, we are glad you are like a parent to us. Sometimes, you are like a mother. Sometimes, you are like a father. Thank you for our parents who care for us daily. Thank you for being like a parent to us and giving us love that never ends. Amen.

36

Love That Does Not Melt

Theme The love of Jesus lasts forever
Scripture John 15:12-17
Object Snow, ice cubes, or a picture of snow

*H*OW MANY OF YOU HAVE had fun playing in the snow? Have you been sledding? Did anyone make a snowman? Has anyone tried snowboarding? *(Adjust this paragraph for your situation.)*

What happens to snow if you bring it inside your house? It melts. You can't keep snow forever. I know many grown-ups are glad snow doesn't last forever!

There is something that lasts forever: the love of Jesus. Jesus invited people to follow him. Jesus and his friends, the disciples, told people that the love of Jesus and the kingdom of God will last forever.

Do you know the best part about the love of Jesus? It is given to each one of us, and it will never melt or disappear like the snow.

We have the great love of Jesus in our lives and share it with other people. Treasure the love Jesus gives to you. Share your love with other people.

Let's pray—

Thank you, Jesus, for your love that doesn't melt like snow or float away in rain. Thank you for love that fills our lives. Help us share your love. Amen.

37

A Gathering
of Hands and Hearts

Theme Our hands and hearts are part of the church
Scripture 1 Corinthians 12:12-26
Object Poster board outline of a church; paper hands

Prepare an outline of a church building. Also cut hand shapes from paper, and place a tape ring on back of each paper hand so it can easily be attached to the church.

HELLO, IT'S GOOD TO SEE YOU! I would like to show you a picture. What is it? You are right; it is a church. Is something missing? Yes, the windows and doors are missing. Let's draw them onto the picture.

Is anything else missing? What about people? People are needed in a church.

I need your help with the picture. I am going to give each of you a hand cut from paper. Attach the hand somewhere in the church.

(Encourage each child to place a hand on the church.) Everyone did a nice job! Now there are lots of hands, lots of people, in the church.

A church is more than a building. A church is also a gathering of people. People come to church to worship God. People also come to find ways to serve in the church. There are many ways to serve.

We can serve through offerings of money and talent. We can serve through offerings of teaching and singing. We can serve through offerings of creativity and keeping our church building nice.

We can serve the larger church—people who are not part of our own church family. However we serve, we use our hands and our hearts filled with love and concern for others.

Every church not only needs a church building, but also helping hands and willing hearts.

Let's pray—

Dear God, thank you for all the people in our church family. Help us to use our helping hands and willing hearts in service for you. Amen.

38

*G*od Doesn't Have Favorites

Theme God doesn't play favorites
Scripture Acts 10:34-43
Object A collection of objects such as seashells or stamps

Bring small collection of items. I used five shells or other pieces from the sea. Be ready to talk about your collection.

I HAVE A COLLECTION I WOULD LIKE to show you. (Talk about your collection.) We have some seashells at our house. We have collected shells at different times when we have been to the ocean.

Let's look at these shells and other pieces from the sea. This is a piece of coral. This is a starfish. This is a sand dollar I found in California.

This unusual shell is my very favorite shell. I found it in South Carolina on an early morning walk along the beach. There had been a storm the night before, and the high waves brought this pretty shell to the beach. I like it so much that I keep it on my desk.

Do any of you collect things? What are some things you collect? Some people collect stamps, rocks, or stuffed animals. There are many different things that people collect.

When we collect things, we often have favorite items. Maybe one particular thing is more important than any of the others. Just like my favorite shell, many people have favorite things in their collection.

Do you know that God doesn't have favorites? God doesn't have favorite things or favorite places or favorite people. God doesn't say, "I like Maggie better than Laban." Or, "I like Fiona better than Kleda." *(Pick some children's names from your gathering of children.)*

God does not prefer one skin color over another or one language over another. God loves each person, and God's love never ends.

Let's pray—

Dear God, thank you for your great love. We are glad that each person is special to you. Help us to be more kind and loving. Amen.

39

A Big Family

Theme There are lots of hands to help in God's family
Scripture Romans 8:14-17
Object Picture that shows two hands

Prepare ahead of time an adult-sized hand and a baby-sized hand cut from construction paper. Keep the hands separate, and tape them together during the story. Or have a parent/grandparent and a baby to demonstrate hand differences.

HELLO THIS FINE MORNING! I brought a hand shape to show you this morning. This is a small hand. Is it smaller than your hands? *(Do a brief comparison.)*

I also have a larger hand. This is about the size of your parents' hands. Do you see how tiny the baby's hand is when compared to the parent's hand?

The hands of parents help children as they grow. Moms and dads use their hands to feed children and care for them. They use their hands to teach children to ride bikes and play ball. They use their hands to help with schoolwork, to make things together, and to help children feel better. Hands are needed for things that happen in a family.

Not only do parents help, but our whole church family also tries to help. We share with one another. We use our hands to comfort each other.

God has been good to our church family. We shake hands. We share hugs and food and cards. We listen to and help one another. Each one of us is an important part of our church family.

All of us are also members of God's larger family. Each one of us is a member of a family that includes all the believers of God. We are loved members of the family of God. God loves each one of us very much. God is like a parent to us. We can talk to God in prayer as we can talk to a mother or father. Being a member of God's family is special.

Let's pray—

Dear God, thank you for all of our families: the family that we live with, our church family, and your larger family. We are glad to be part of your family. Amen.

40
*W*hat Is Your Talent?

Theme We all have different gifts from God
Scripture Romans 12:6-8
Objects Variety of toys in a bag

Use the italicized sections of information to adapt this story time for your group.

WHAT A JOY TO SEE ALL OF YOU! As I look at you, I think I see many children who like to play. Am I right? Do you like to play?

Playing is fun. Playing helps you use your imagination. When you play together, you learn that some children do some things well while other children do other things well. You are learning what talents your friends have.

(Bring a bag with a variety of items that would demonstrate a talent. Try to have an item that mentions a talent for each child. If you have a large group of children, you may want to make this more general.)

When you learn that a friend does something well, encourage your friend and mention what your friend does well. For instance, I could encourage you by saying:

(Use your bag of "talents" at this point.)

1) *blocks:* I know that Joel builds nicely; 2) *soccer ball:* I know that Isaac, Andrew, and Zeb play soccer; 3) *yel-*

low crayon: I know that Sophie likes to draw, and her favorite color is yellow; 4) *sign language book:* I know that Olivia and Fiona help Cecelia with sign language; 5) *a wildlife picture:* I know that Aaron likes to learn about nature.

(If you decide to be more general, here are some examples.)

1) *pencils, paper:* I know that some of you like school very much; 2) *music books:* Some of you enjoy singing; 3) *ball:* Some of you like to play ball.

Today in our worship service, we are thinking about what it means to call people to ministry. We are thinking about what talents people have, about what things they do well.

God has given each one of us special talents. Some people have special talents for activities like preaching, teaching, or caring for other people.

God wants us to use our talents in many ways. When you grow up, maybe you will become the pastor of a church. Even if you don't become a pastor, you can use your talents for God. Keep encouraging one another, and keep finding ways to use the talents God gave you.

Let's pray—

Dear God, you have given each of us many talents. Help us to learn about our talents. Help us to encourage one another to use our talents for your kingdom. Amen.

41

The Language of Love

Theme We'are all different and need to love one another
Scripture Romans 13:8-10
Object People saying "love" in different languages

Do you know people in your congregation who speak different languages? Arrange for them to join you during the children's time. Ask them to say the word "love" in the different languages they speak.

I'VE HEARD THAT THE MOST IMPORTANT word in our language is this one: the word *love*. We often talk about love around Valentine's Day, but we think about love every day.

We love our friends. We love our family members. Most of the time it's easy to love others, but sometimes brothers and sisters fight. They may even think they don't like one another.

Jesus taught a lot about love. He said, "This I command you, love one another." Jesus tells us to put love in an important spot in our lives. We need to care for and love each other.

I have asked several people from our congregation to join me. Each of these people knows how to say the word love in a different language. Listen as they say the word love. *(Take time for each person to tell the children briefly about the language being spoken. A variation of this would be to create a poster with the word* love *written in various languages. Introduce the different words to the children.)*

Even though all of these words sound different, they all mean the same thing—love.

I hope each of you tries to put love in an important spot in your life. Jesus teaches us to love everyone. That means family members, friends, people we will meet, and even people we may never meet.

Let's pray—

Dear God, thank you so much for your wonderful gift of love. Help us to put love in an important spot in our lives, so that we may easily love one another. Amen.

42

A Rainbow of People

Theme Our world has many different people
Scripture 1 Corinthians 12
Object Crepe paper strips, paper plate, stapler

Ahead of time, prepare strips of crepe paper in different colors. These can represent various groups of people.)

HOW MANY OF YOU HAVE ever seen a rainbow? Rainbows are beautiful. Rainbows happen only occasionally. The sun and the rain need to be just right to make a rainbow.

We also see another kind of rainbow in our world—a rainbow of people. There are many different people in our world. Not only do they have different colors of skin, but people also have many different talents.

(As you mention the different talents, staple the strips of crepe paper to the paper plate to create a "rainbow.")

Many people are leaders. They help people along the way.

Many people are creative. They share their talents of music and art and other creations with us.

Many people are teachers. They share their knowledge with other people and help them to learn.

Many people are good at making other people feel better. Sometimes, their words help us feel better. Sometimes, their actions help us feel better.

Many people are good listeners. They listen carefully to other people. All of us are called to share God's love and peace with other people.

Our world is a more beautiful place because of this rainbow of people. We help to keep our world beautiful by sharing the talents God has given us, by sharing the wonderful love of God with other people.

Through our words and actions, let's find ways to share God's love and peace with one another.

Let's pray—

Dear God, thank you for the rainbow of people in our world. Help us to share your love and peace with other people. Amen.

43
On God's Team

Theme We are members of God's team
Scripture Ephesians 2:11-22
Object Various items with team logos

I'M GLAD EACH OF YOU IS A PART of our church
family. This morning I have some things in this bag
to show you.

*(Adapt these next few sentences to speak about your
team items.)* First, I have a gray shirt. Who recognizes
this design on the front the shirt? Yes, this is Joel's t-
ball shirt. I know that some of you also play t-ball.

I have another shirt. This is Aaron's baseball shirt,
and here is a hat that says PSU. What does PSU stand
for? It stands for Penn State; you are right. This is an of-
ficial Penn State baseball hat.

How about this? This is a Huntingdon Bearcats
football shirt. Where is this sweatshirt from? You are
right; it is from Juniata College.

All of these things are pieces needed to be a member of a team. Some of you may have a special hat or
shirt if you are a member of a scout group. We wear
different things to show we are members of different
groups or teams.

We are all members of God's team or family. God
has a worldwide family. Skin color doesn't matter; language doesn't matter; and what we wear doesn't mat-

ter. Everyone is a member of God's worldwide family. Even someone you may not like very well is a member of God's family

We may not wear special hats and shirts to show we are members of God's team, but our actions will show that we belong to God.

Each day do things that God would want you to do. Be kind and helpful. Care for one another. Show love to other people. You are a member of God's team.

Let's pray—

Dear God, we are glad that we can be members of your team. Thanks for your love and for being with us always. Amen.

44

*W*e Need Jesus

Theme We need Jesus
Scripture Colossians 1:15-20
Object Pictures of various items or actual items

*I*HAVE SOME THINGS IN THIS BAG that I would like
to show you. Each of these things represents something that we need. Let's look together, and think
about how we need these items.

We need food to grow strong and be healthy.

We need water for our bodies to stay healthy.

We need families; people to love and care for us;
people to help us when we are sad; people to be happy
with us when we are happy.

We need houses; places to shelter us from storms
and cold weather.

We need clothes to wear.

We need medicine to help us feel better when we
become sick.

We need a Bible to learn about Jesus Christ.

We need all of these things to be healthy and safe
and happy. Especially, we need Jesus in our lives. Jesus
promises to be with us always. Jesus, as God's Son, is
in our world. He is with each one of us.

We have a wonderful gift because each one of us
has been given the love of Jesus. Jesus' love never
ends, and that is amazing. Jesus knows each one of us,

and that is amazing. Jesus is willing to help each of us, and that is amazing. We are thankful to have this amazing Jesus in our lives.

Let's pray—
Dear Jesus, thank you for being so amazing. We are glad for your love and care. We are glad that you are so great that you know each person and that you care for each person. Amen.

45
All People Everywhere

Theme We are asked to pray for all people
Scripture 1 Timothy 2:1-7
Object Globe

THIS MORNING I BROUGHT A GLOBE. It is a model of our world. It shows land shapes and water. The names of countries and bodies of water are printed on the globe. We live here. *(Point.)* Our place on this globe is tiny compared to all the world's places.

People live all over the world. People of the world are different in many ways. We have different houses, foods, and styles of clothing.

We have different cultures. But we are all the same because we are members of God's worldwide family. God loves all people. God created every person in God's image. God loves each of us.

God asks us to pray for other people in this worldwide family. We pray people will have enough food, safe places to live, and health. We pray they will know God's wonderful love.

Let's spin the globe, and pray for people in different parts of the world. *(Spin globe and name area.)*

Let's pray—
Dear God, We pray for people in. . . . We pray for people in. . . . We pray for people everywhere. Amen.

46
Doing Is a Necessary Part of Life

Theme Let us be doers as well as hearers of God's word
Scripture James 1:22-25
Object Giant cookie to share with the children

*H*OW MANY OF YOU LIKE to help bake cookies for your family? Baking together with mom or dad is fun, isn't it?

First, you need to follow the recipe. You mix the ingredients and create the batter. Are you finished? Can you eat the cookies? No! You must bake the cookies.

Before you can eat them, you have to do the baking. If you don't do the baking, the cookies will not be completed.

It is the same with being a Christian. We come to the worship service. We listen to the Scripture, and we hear the sermon. We listen to special music, and we sing hymns.

We listen to all these things; but unless we put our words into action, we aren't doing all that God wants us to do. We can't just know what God wants us to do. We need to do what God wants us to do.

Now I have something to share with you. We talked about baking cookies at the beginning of our time together.

I brought a giant cookie to be shared. I am sharing it with you because sharing and caring for others is a great way to do service in God's kingdom. *(Is there a youth class who could bake the giant cookie as a service project? This is a good way to involve others in "doing the word." See the recipe below.)*

Giant Cookie Recipe
½ cup brown sugar, ½ cup white sugar, 1 egg, 1 ¼ cup flour, 1 tsp. baking soda, ½ cup margarine, ½ cup peanut butter, 1 tsp. vanilla, ½ tsp. salt, 1 cup chocolate chips, 1 T. water
Preheat oven to 350 degrees. Mix sugars, margarine, peanut butter, egg, vanilla. Add dry ingredients. Mix well. Add chocolate chips. Stir. If batter seems stiff, add 1 tablespoon of water. Pat dough onto greased pizza tin. Bake 12-15 minutes.

Let's pray—
Dear God, help us to keep our eyes and ears open to know how we can do things for you and share with others. Amen.

47

The Hands of Peace

Theme We are called to carry on Jesus' mission for peace
Scripture James 3:13-18
Object Banner with handprints

For story-time emphasis on peace, I made a banner with each child's handprint. The banner heading says, "These are the hands that make for peace." The story can be used without the banner. Draw attention, though, to each child's hands, and remind them that they have the hands of peacemakers.

TODAY, WE ARE THINKING OF PEACE. I don't mean piece like a piece of candy. We are thinking of another kind of peace—the kind of peace that Jesus worked for. When you hear the word *peace,* what do you think about? *(Wait for the children's responses.)*

You have good ideas about peace. Peace means many things, doesn't it? It is not just absence of war.

Peace can mean quietness and calmness. Peace can mean being well. Peace can mean being able to work out problems in a loving way. We want to have peace in our lives.

Because Jesus worked for peace, it is important for us to know about peace. Jesus had a mission for peace. He wanted goodness for all the people. Because we are followers of Jesus, we too need to work for peace.

I read something that a famous man named Gandhi said. Gandhi, who was a wise peacemaker, said that "If

110

we are to reach real peace in this world, we have to begin with the children."

What Gandhi meant by that is that each one of you can be a peacemaker. In yourself you can have peace. With your family and your friends, you can have peace. You can be a peacemaker.

I made something to help us remember that we can all be peacemakers. Who can read the words on the banner? You have the hands that can work for peace. Not only can you use your hands to work for peace, but you can also use your hearts and minds.

Each one of you can use your hands, your heart, and your mind to be peaceful. Let's pray that God will help each one of us to be peacemakers.

Let's pray—

Dear God, we know how important peace is. Guide us to use our hearts, minds, and hands to work for peace. Amen.

48

Growing Strong

Theme We grow as we learn more about God
Scripture 1 Peter 2:2-10
Object Seedlings

IT'S SPRINGTIME! How many of you have planted
seeds this spring? Have any of you helped plant a
garden? This is the time of year to plant and care for
seeds and little plants.

Later this summer, we will have vegetables from
seeds planted this spring. We can also enjoy the beauty
of flowers from seeds that have been planted.

This morning I want to show you some little plants.
(Adjust this paragraph to refer to your seedlings.) This is
called a "window greenhouse."

These plants grew from seeds that were planted
several weeks ago. It is time for the plants to be re-
planted into bigger pots. What did these seeds need to
grow into plants? Yes, they needed things like soil,
water, sunshine, and time.

All of those things are needed for these seeds to
grow. As the plants grow, we replant them into bigger
pots. Finally, we plant them outside. All the time, they
still need soil, water, and sunshine. They need time to
grow bigger and to produce vegetables.

We are like seeds when we are growing as
Christians. As we grow in following Jesus, we need

some things. We need to hear important messages from the Bible. We need to learn about Jesus in church school and during our worship time.

We grow in following Jesus as we spend time with other Christians. We sing songs, pray, and study the Bible to help us to learn about Jesus.

As we do these things, we are growing stronger just like these seeds. Do you know that all of us are still growing as Christians? Yes. All of us are growing—not just children.

Even your parents and other adults are growing as Christians. Each day, try to find a way that you can grow into a stronger follower of Jesus.

Let's pray—

Dear God, thank you for all the plants that are growing. Thank you that they help to make our world beautiful. Help each one of us to grow into a stronger follower of Jesus. Amen.

49

A Cup of Cold Water

Theme As we serve others, we are serving God
Scripture Matthew 10:40-42
Object Clear pitcher of water and cups

This story is particularly effective if the day is warm!

*F*OR OUR STORY TIME TODAY, I need you to use your imagination. Maybe you would like to close your eyes while you imagine.

Imagine that it is a very warm day, and you are outside playing. You've been doing some exciting things on this warm summer day. You've been swinging. You've been playing a ball game with some friends. You have even climbed a tree.

It's been a fun day, but the temperature has been very warm. You've been playing for such a long time! You realize that you are hot and thirsty.

What would you like to have? What would make you feel better? *(Wait for their responses.)* Yes, a cold drink, a cup of cold water, would be wonderful.

There is a verse in the Bible where Jesus says "Whoever gives a cup of cold water to these little ones will not lose their reward." We know how good a cup of cold water tastes when we really need it.

The cup of cold water does help us to feel better, but actually Jesus isn't talking just about a cup of cold water. Jesus is using the water as a way of also teaching us to help one another.

Jesus tells us we should find ways to serve others. As we serve one another, we are doing what Jesus wants us to do. We are honoring Jesus.

Each day try to find a way to help someone. Maybe you can make a card for someone who is feeling sad. Maybe you can help your parents with a project they are doing. Maybe you can play a game with someone. Or maybe you can give someone a drink of cold water. Let's share a drink of water right now.

Let's pray—

Dear God, thank you for people who help us. Help us to be able to see how we can help other people. Amen.

50

*P*oint the Way
Advent

Theme Some events and some people point us to Jesus
Scripture Luke 3:1-14
Object Poster board candles for each child

Prepare ahead of time a candle shape from poster board for each child. Print the word "prepare" on the candle. Attach some yarn so it can hang as an ornament.

GOOD MORNING! I am glad to see all of you. We are in the midst of Advent. Each week we light the candles as a reminder that we are preparing for Jesus to come.

Another way to say we are "preparing" is to say we are "getting ready." We are getting ready for Jesus to come. Some things and activities help us get ready.

Like these Advent candles, these things and activities point us to Christmas. They help us focus on getting ready for Jesus' coming.

If your family is using an Advent calendar, the calendar helps point you to Christmas.

The cards we receive in the mail point us to Christmas.

The songs we sing point us to Christmas.

The star in the sky pointed the shepherds toward the baby Jesus.

Sometimes, people point us toward Jesus and Christmas. In the Bible we read about a man named John the Baptist.

John pointed the people toward Jesus. He spent time in the desert and ate wild honey and locusts. That is an unusual diet!

John preached that we should focus on Jesus and prepare the way for the coming of Jesus. John's words are still good for us today. John preached that we should live good lives, that we should share and be honest. John preached that we should follow Jesus.

I have a tree ornament for each of you. This is a candle shape that has the word "prepare" printed on it. Hang this candle on your tree so it will help point you to Christmas.

Let's pray—

Dear God, thank you for the things and the people that point us to Christmas. Help us to prepare for the coming of Jesus. Amen.

51

O Come Let Us Adore Him

Theme We give adoration to Jesus
Scripture Luke 1:47-55
Object Christmas cards showing manger scene

WHAT SPECIAL DAY IS COMING this week? *(Expect a joyful response!)* I knew you would know! Christmas is just ___ days away. Whose birthday do we celebrate on Christmas? I knew you would know that, too. It is Jesus' birthday.

This morning I have several Christmas cards that I would like to show you. I like receiving Christmas cards in the mail.

It is fun to see who sent them, and I like to see the picture on the card. Let's talk about what we see on the cards. *(All the cards should be pictures of the Nativity. Let the children tell what they see in the pictures: Baby Jesus in a manger, Mary and Joseph, angels, shepherds, people kneeling, people giving gifts, etc. Draw the children to the conclusion that people are adoring Jesus.)*

All the people are adoring Jesus. They know how special Jesus is. They are kneeling, giving gifts, or in some way showing how happy they are that Jesus has been born. They are worshipping Jesus.

We, too, are glad that Jesus was born. We show Jesus that we are glad for his birth by celebrating it at Christmas. We adore and worship Jesus just like the people pictured on the Christmas cards. Every Sunday when we come to church, we are worshipping Jesus.

I will give each of you one of these cards to remind you of the manger scene. Put this card in a special place. Maybe you could put it on the refrigerator or by your bed or maybe on a branch of your Christmas tree. When you look at it, remember to say, "Jesus, I am glad you were born."

Let's pray—

Dear God, thank you for this special day when Jesus was born. We are happy because of his birth. Amen.

52
A Light for Us

Theme Jesus is the light of the world
Scripture John 1:1-14
Object Candle

Draw attention to the Christ candle if one is included in your worship. If not, bring a candle to the time with the children.

*H*AVE YOU NOTICED THAT each time we begin our worship service someone brings a candle to our communion table? It is called "The Candle of Christ's Presence." What do you think that means? *(Accept and encourage their responses.)*

The candle is a symbol to remind us that Jesus is with us always. Jesus brings light to our lives.

Jesus is called the light of the world. Jesus gives us light. We are thankful to have the light of Jesus in our lives.

Believing in Jesus brightens our lives because we have an example to follow. Jesus gives us the best example possible.

He cared for other people; he didn't collect material things; he worked for peace. Jesus showed us the way to live. Jesus gave us light for our lives.

We can share that wonderful light, the light of Jesus, with other people. We can tell other people about Jesus. Most of all, other people can see Jesus by our actions. When we care for other people and live the way Jesus wants us to live, we are sharing the light of Jesus with other people.

Let's pray—
　Dear God, thank you for the shining light of Jesus. Guide us as we follow that light, and help us to help other people see the light of Jesus. Amen.

Sample
Prayer Card for Lesson 22

Our Father who art in heaven,
God is never too far to hear our prayers. God is like a loving parent who will always listen.

hallowed be thy name,
We are promising to respect God's name and not make fun of it. We are promising to love God and let our lives show that love.

thy kingdom come, thy will be done on earth as it is in heaven.
We are saying we trust God in our lives. We want to do what God wants us to do. Sometimes that is not easy, but we promise to try to do our best.

Give us this day our daily bread;
We know that God is the giver of all good things. We know that God gives us what we need. We have food, a home, and people that care for us.

And forgive our debts as we forgive our debtors;
God gives us his forgiveness freely. We only need to ask God to forgive us. God asks us to forgive people who have hurt us.

And lead us not into temptation, but deliver us from evil.
We are asking God to guide and lead us.

For thine is the kingdom, and the power, and the glory forever, Amen.
We are praising God and saying, "God you are great. You are wonderful." We can always praise God.

Index of Scripture References

Scripture reference	Book #
Genesis 1	1
Genesis 1:26-27	2, 3
Genesis 2:7	1
Genesis 24:50-61	3
Exodus 14:5-15	1
Exodus 20:3	1
Exodus 20:3-6	2
Deuteronomy 4:9-14	2
Deuteronomy 6:4-9	3
Joshua 24:14-25	3
Ruth 1:16-17	2
1 Samuel 3:1-20	1
1 Samuel 8:4-20	2
1 Kings 19:9-14	3
Psalm 1	3
Psalm 19:14	1
Psalm 22	3
Psalm 23	3
Psalm 27:1-9	2
Psalm 29	2
Psalm 57:1	1, 2
Psalm 90:17	1
Psalm 119:33-40	1
Psalm 119:105	3
Psalm 121:3-4	1

Ephesians 5:1-2	2
Philippians 1:3-11	1
Philippians 2:3-4	1
Philippians 2:1-11	2
Philippians 4:1-9	1
Colossians 1:15-20	3
1 Thessalonians 3:13	1
1 Timothy 2:1-7	3
2 Timothy 1:1-14	1
Hebrews 4:9-13	1
James 1:17	2
James 1:22-23	2
James 1:22-25	3
James 3:13-18	3
James 5:7-8	2
James 5:13-16	1
1 Peter 1:3-9	3
1Peter 2:4-5	2
1 Peter 2:2-10	3
1 Peter 5:7	1
1 John 4:7-8	1
Revelation 3:20	2

The Author

Donna McKee Rhodes, an ordained Church of the Brethren minister, is Pastor of Nurture at Stone Church of the Brethren in Huntingdon, Pennsylvania. As a 1984 graduate of Juniata College, she received a B.S. in early childhood and elementary education. She also completed the Church of the Brethren Training in Ministry program.

Donna's Christian education experience includes roles as teacher, consultant, developer of educational material, and author. Among her writings are *Little Stories for Little Children* (Herald Press, 1995), which won a Silver Angel award; *More Little Stories for Little Children* (Herald Press, 1997), and a segment of *Jubilee! God's Good News*, curriculum for children in Anabaptist churches.

Other publishing projects include articles for the magazine *Common Ground* as well as a variety of photographs. Donna is editor of the Church of the Brethren Association of Christian Educator's (CoBACE) denominational newsletter.

Born in Mifflin County, Pennsylvania, Donna now lives in Huntingdon with her husband Loren, Juniata College professor of computer science, and their three children, Erica, Aaron, and Joel. Donna enjoys music, counted cross-stitch, photography, and the activities of her children.